T0194020

THE ATLANTIC CITY: CLUB HARLEM

AuthorHouse™
1663 Liberty Drive
Bloomington, IN 47403
www.authorhouse.com
Phone: 833-262-8899

This book is printed on acid-free paper.

ISBN: 978-1-7283-6598-5 (sc)
ISBN: 978-1-7283-6597-8 (e)

Print information available on the last page.

Published by AuthorHouse 02/24/2021

authorHOUSE®

Contents

Walter D Palmer Leadership School

C urrently W.D. Palmer is the founder and director of the W.D. Palmer Foundation (est. 1955), a repository of information on racism in health, education, employment, housing, courts, prisons, higher education, military, government, politics, law, banking, insurance, etc. He is also the founder of the Black People's University of Philadelphia Freedom School (1955), which was the grassroots organizing and training center for grassroots community and political leadership in Philadelphia and nationally. These organizations were run as nonprofit unincorporated associations from 1955 until 1980 when the Palmer Foundation received its 501(c)(3) federal tax exemption status.

W.D. Palmer has also been a professor, teaching American Racism at the University of Pennsylvania since the 1960s and today he is a member of the Presidents Commission on 1619 four-hundred-year anniversary of African slavery in America. Professor Palmer has been a social activist leading the fight against racial injustice for over sixty years in Philadelphia and around the nation. In 1980, he led the fight for parental school choice which helped Pennsylvania governor Thomas Ridge get a law passed in 1997. Most recently in 2020, Philadelphia honored him for 60 years of fighting for social justice throughout the country.

In 2005, W.D. Palmer created the Walter D. Palmer Leadership Charter School, which borrowed eleven million dollars to build a two-story, 55,000 square foot building on two acres of land in North Philadelphia and acquired the Saint Bartholomew School for its middle and high school students. The school grew from 300 elementary school students in 2000, to 200 preschoolers and over 1,000 kindergarten to 12th graders by 2012.

W.D. Palmer commissioned a muralist to paint over 400 pre-selected portraits on the school walls, corridors, and stairwells, along with 25 individual 15-foot murals in the gymnasium. The Walter D. Palmer Leadership School recruited at-risk children from 17 of the poorest zip codes in Philadelphia, most of whom were 300% below the poverty line. Despite this, the school boasted a 95% daily attendance, 100% graduation rate, and 100% post graduate placement in two or four year colleges, trade, technology schools, or military service until the school's closing in 2015.

My Relationship to Atlantic City Club Harlem

by Walter D. Palmer

I was born in Atlantic City, New Jersey to Walter Palmer and Hanah Byard. I was the second of eight children, first living on Virginia Avenue, then Rider Avenue as the family grew. Atlantic City Blacks were segregated to the north side of the city towards the bay and white people were segregated to the south side towards the ocean.

My father, like most Blacks in the town, could not find work because of the seasonal work and pervading racial discrimination. Atlantic City Northside was a self-contained community with businesses, schools, churches, lawyers, two doctors, and a nurse. This was complemented by a number of successful bars, eateries, and nightclubs, many of which were located on Kentucky Avenue. Many of the bars included Timbuctu, Walt's, Ike's, Mark IV, Red Klutz, Top Hat, and Silk Hat. Popular eateries included Mom's Kitchen, Kelly's, Johnson's, Sapps, Fishery, Jerry's Barbecue, Grace's Little Belmont, Goldie's Bar, Wondergarden and Rex's Sub Shop.

The main attraction night clubs on Kentucky Avenue were Goldie's Little Belmont and the famous Club Harlem (1893 to 1993). Originally named Fitzgerald Ballroom (1893 to 1935), it was built as a haven and refuge for Blacks in Atlantic City because they were cut out of all other social, educational, political, and economic life in Atlantic City.

My father, mother, aunts, and uncles would frequent Club Harlem over the years because it was the epicenter of Atlantic City Black life and culture. When I was seven years old my father moved our family to Philadelphia and we lived in a two room flat in the back of my stepsister's beauty shop. We left Atlantic City in the 1940s and would return every summer for the next 40 years. In 1985, I went back to Atlantic City to work on the recall of a sitting mayor and stayed to organize and direct the election of Mayor James Ursy, the city's first Black mayor. The historic Club Harlem was at the center of Ursy's election campaign.

Acknowledgments

———————●———————

Since the inception of the Black People's University Freedom School, we have designed all learning materials to be student driven. We encourage students from elementary, middle, high school, and college to research, write, produce, and publish our work. Therefore, all of W.D. Palmer Publishing's written work will reflect a strategy that encourages student leadership.

In 1985, I tried to buy Club Harlem and get the city to declare it a
historic landmark. Unfortunately, this effort failed.
In 1993, the Club was torn down, but a number of entertainer
photographs and about 10% of the brick façade was saved.

- Walter D. Palmer

A piece of this historic memorabilia can be acquired to complement this book by contacting the following:
thewdpalmerfoundation@gmail.com
(267) 738-1588
PO Box 22692
Philadelphia, PA 19110

Notice

———•———

Any proceeds derived from the sales or donations of this book will go towards the development of additional leadership and educational curriculum, as well as training materials for our at-risk children and their families living in marginal communities.

This book is dedicated to the Atlantic City Afros who fought to make a difference and brought change to Atlantic City in the face of adversity.

(Leroy "Pop" Williams, the founder, and Ben Alten, the manager, of Club Harlem)

Primary Organizer: W.D. Palmer
Secondary Organizer: Nicole Felicetti
Marketing Organizer: Justin Pita

Where to go for a piece of the Club Harlem brick facade:
thewdpalmerfoundation@gmail.com
(267) 738-1588
PO Box 22692 Philadelphia, PA 19110
https://www.speakerservices.com/walter-d-palmer/

Atlantic City

"The World's Greatest Playground"

Kentucky Avenue and the Club that helped save a people, "A hidden American treasure, tragedy, and legacy"

Atlantic City and Absecon Island was initially inhabited by the Lenepe and Absegami Indians who had roamed the wooded area of great white beaches and Great Ocean for over 400 years before Christ. The white settlers didn't come into the area until the 1600s and eventually bought Absecon Island for 40 cents per acre. The natives always believed that there was something magical and healthy about the sunshine, beaches, and ocean, so they would run hundreds of miles to the beach and ocean.

In the 1850s a 22-year-old doctor from England named Jonathan Pitney petitioned the New Jersey state legislature for a charter incorporating Atlantic City into the New Jersey commonwealth. After several years of petitioning the state, they awarded Pitney a charter for Atlantic City in 1854, finally convincing them that the native claims about the area were true. Between 1854 and 1954 Atlantic City would make history by creating the first boardwalk, first Ferris wheel, first submarine, first air show, world's largest organ, and first playground in the world, all which attracted millions of visitors to these shores. During the period between 1854 and 1856, Atlantic City also received the right to build a railroad, appealing to people from all across America and the world.

Although railroad development peaked ten years before the end of the Civil War and the end of formal slavery in America, many Blacks had migrated to Atlantic City from the south via Chester and Philadelphia, Pennsylvania. Though Blacks helped build the Boardwalks, they weren't welcome to walk on them or the beaches. The same goes for the hotels, kitchens, and dining rooms, and for many years they were not allowed to sleep in the beds, work in the kitchens, or dine in the eateries.

Despite also helping to build the night clubs, Black patrons were initially not allowed to perform in or attend any of the shows. Though they helped build the hospitals, they were given segregated rooms or limited to giving birth at home by a midwife. Racial segregation was a customary practice in the entertainment world all over the United States and forced Blacks to build their own hotels, eateries, bars, and night clubs.

Larry with Josephine Baker

*Larry with Walter Winchell at the 1964
Democratic Convention in Atlantic City*

In Louisiana, the Blacks had Basin Street to create their own entertainment center. Philadelphia was bustling with entertainment options like the Royal Theatre (1919-1970), Fays Theatre (1919-1963), Pearl Theatres (1927-1963), and the Powelton Bar. New York, mostly famously, had the Apollo Theatre. In response to the racial discrimination in Atlantic City, the Fitzgeralds, a Black family, built the Fitzgerald Auditorium and Ballroom at 30 North Kentucky Avenue in 1893. This auditorium was used by Blacks to host roller skating, dances, dinners, shows, weddings, showers, and funeral repasts, and serve as the center of Black professional and political organizing. In 1930, the dancehall was acquired by Leroy "Pop" Williams a local Atlantic City number banker, who had also bought 32 North Kentucky Avenue. In 1935, Leroy Williams and his brother Cliff Williams bought the Fitzgerald's Auditorium and named it Club Harlem.

Since racial discrimination was in every aspect of American life, including entertainment, it was a catalyst that produced some of the most unique and original music, art, dance, and drama, in the United States and around the world, specifically by Black Americans. "Pop" Williams and his brother Cliff attracted and recruited many of the greatest artists from all over the country. Later, with the addition of the musical impresario Larry "Smart Affairs" Steele, they engineered and steered their club to be one of the greatest Black professional entertainment centers in the world. Performing legends like Billy Eckstein, Billy Paul, Sarah Vaughan, Ella Fitzgerald, Jimmy Smith, "Slappy" White, Redd Foxx, Cab Calloway, Pearl Bailey, Bill Bailey, Billy Daniels, Sam Cooke, Jackie "Moms" Mabley and a Smart Affairs Dance Chorus directed by Larry Steele graced the Club Harlem stage.

Larry with the Great Lady of the Entertainment World, Lena Horne, 1956)

The 'Champ' Joe Louis awards citations to Sammy Davis, Jr. and Larry, 1963

Lola Falana

*Larry Steele with Nat King Cole and
Lieutenant John D. Chamberlain, 1963*

Before "Pop" Williams went to prison for income tax evasion, he took on a partner named Ben Alten, a white businessman in the entertainment world who would manage and direct the club, expressly as "Pop" Williams had dictated, until his return.

Kentucky Avenue entertainment ran one block from Atlantic Avenue to Arctic Avenue where Club Harlem was the epicenter for Black entertainment in Atlantic City. Other notable musical bars in the area included Goldie's, Grace's Little Belmont, Wonder Garden, and the Timbuctu on Arctic Avenue. The eateries on the Avenue included Sapp's Barbecue, Jerry's Barbecue, Russell's Barbecue, the Fishery, and Johnson's restaurant. Because there were many families living on that one block of Kentucky Avenue, there was a host of other businesses and services. Some of the daytime business were London's Pharmacy, Carter's Printing, Rex Sub House, Kensington Furniture, Wagonheim's Meat Market, Acardie's Fish Market, Hatcher's Cleaners, B&B Rooms, and Reuben's Cleaners.

Although the history of Atlantic City and the Atlantic City Northside focused a lot on the boardwalk, Steel Pier, Gardner's Basin, and Kentucky Avenue were important cultural centers, too. Atlantic City in its heyday had seen its population rise to 75,000 people who lived from Maine Avenue to Jackson Avenue, and from the Atlantic Ocean to the Bay.

Lou Rawls Smart Affairs, 1967

Larry with Satchmo Louis Armstrong, 1951

[insert CH 12] (Sam Cooke)

"Larry Steele is a high-principled man who refuses to compromise his honor. (It isn't easy in a spot such as his). Quite often in his 'formative years', his talent and his imagination out-raced his finances; and backers were hard to find. Until relatively recent years, there always were club-owners who slammed doors in his face ("Personally I'd like to present your show, but I'm afraid my customers wouldn't appreciate your type revue"). The total hurt that wells up in the heart of an American like Larry (who merely hap-pens to be colored) is almost enough to make a man go downtown and jump off City Hall. But Larry's flesh isn't weak, nor is his spirit. He has always been wedded to show business for better or for worse. When things were worse, he did the best he could, summoning the last ounce of the ingenuity he possessed to make ends meet. When things got better, he was ready for prosperity. But, even today, he isn't a man who takes success for granted. A lesser man—thinking of headline triumphs from 'coast-to-coast' and from country-to-country—would be prone to stick out his chest like a peacock and brag. "I've got it made." Not Larry. He came up the hard way. Which is the true way. In the crucible of trials and tribulations, he is confirmed as a professional."

Grand Finale, Smart Affairs 1957,
Dunes Hotel, Las Vegas

The Kentucky Avenue entertainment block was open for business 24 hours a day; a regular street by day, but an open, less regulated street by night. Aside from all the great food, drinking, and entertainment provided by the avenue, there was an underground economy of speakeasies, prostitution, selling stolen goods, dice shooting, skin games, boot liquor, fencing, and drugs.

In response to the segregation around the Atlantic City Northside from 1854 to 1954, the Black community built what was like a city within a city to accommodate their livelihoods. By 1930, Black residents on the north side of Atlantic City were becoming more politically connected as they built churches of every major denomination, civic and benevolent societies like the Elks, and the Black Professional board of trades to contribute to the ever-growing Black population. After years of denial in jobs within in the police and fire departments, schools, and restaurants, they built their own restaurants and stores, bars, and clubs on the north side. Some of the more prominent bars were Reggie's, Hi Hat and Top Hat, Daddy Lou's, Ike's Corner, and Walt's Bar.

Larry with Mabel Scott, Maurice Rocco, and Pigmeat Markham are welcomed to Australia by the Governor General

In the underground economy, the Black community wrote and played numbers, shot dice, rented rooms, played cards, held red-light and blue-light dances, hosted rent parties, and ran pool games and speakeasies. Most of the revenue that Blacks earned came from these parties and games, soul food, and alcohol. In many cases, these revenues were the basis for many Blacks across America to elevate the next generation to higher education and home ownership. Today in Atlantic City, many Blacks enjoy employment in the schools, fire and police departments, hospitals, the post office, department stores, clubs and casinos, as well as business ownership. Today Blacks own homes and businesses in every section of Atlantic City, from northeast Inlet to Bungalow Park--west side, Monroe Park, Venice Park, Lagoon, Chelsea, and Chelsea Heights.

Marvin Gaye

With the exception of the Atlantic City Afros in the mid to late 1960's, Atlantic City did not experience any long-term involvement in the civil rights or Black Power movements. With the emergence of large populations of Indian, Bangladesh, Pakistani, Caribbean, Haitian, African, Spanish/Latino/a, European, and Asians, the existing Black population aged and moved away. Over the course of the following 10-20 years, the Black community that founded the entertainment hub diminished and the legacy of their businesses lessened. By the 1960's, Atlantic City entered an economic downturn and lost a large portion of its population. In order to address ongoing issues, casino gambling was proposed as a solution for the dwindling economy. Although North Jersey rejected gambling twice, Atlantic City eventually led South Jersey in creating a final referendum for gambling in the city.

Before 1978, politicians and casino operators made extravagant assurances to Atlantic City residents that they would share in the new casino revenue. However, after the casinos were successful, politicians retracted all the promises they had made to the Atlantic City residents. The arrival of casinos and their lucrative year-round jobs, food, drinks, excursions, and free chips to gamble had a destructive impact on the livelihood of the Black Northside. Many of the bars, clubs, restaurants, bed and breakfast establishments, clothing, grocery, variety, and convenience stores closed their doors unable to compete with the large, corporate casinos. Club Harlem suffered from inability to contend with the casinos as well, but it was a tragic incident that initiated its impending decline.

For over a hundred years the white gangsters had an unwritten code where they agreed that killing in Atlantic City was prohibited. However, in 1972, the Club Harlem was dealt a fatal blow when some Black gangsters (the Black Mafia) from Philadelphia had a shootout during the Easter evening show. Unfortunately, several people were killed and 11 patrons were wounded.

In 1990, Ben Alten agreed to sell the Club for $250,000. I took an investment proposal to James Usry, the first African-American Mayor of Atlantic City, but unfortunately he was unable to get political or financial support to sponsor the club. I did, however, return to Atlantic City frequently between 1982 and 2002 to run Usry's political campaigns and help build a Black Government in the city. I was called on to run successful campaigns for committee people, city council, board of education, freeholder, state assembly, state senate, and gubernatorial candidates as well as reorganize the Atlantic County Democratic organization.

Larry Steele with Mrs. Robert S. Vann and the late Daisy Lampkins, congratulating George Kirby, 1951)

(Larry Steele with Harry Belafonte, 1961)

Although there had been a number of attempts to restore Club Harlem by Benny Alten and different entrepreneurs, revitalization was unsuccessful. Club Harlem was demolished in 1993. Fortunately, I was able to retrieve a number of entertainer's pictures and over ten percent of the brick facade of Club Harlem.

This has been a brief history of the Atlantic City Northside, Kentucky Avenue, and Club Harlem, as well as a collection of original photos from Club Harlem's past, including photos of "Pop" Williams and Benny Alten, Larry Steele, and many of the entertainers that performed at Club Harlem in its heyday. Please email thewdpalmerfoundation@gmail.com for a piece of the Club Harlem brick façade. This all is offered to you as a tribute to one of America's hidden treasures and greatest legacies.

By A.S. "Doc" Young

The men who make the world go 'round, who pioneer, who create the action, who sustain the glories of indomitable enterprise, who boot their own long-shot projects home as winners, belong to a special, dynamic breed.

They are dreamers, but they are not idle dreamers. They are, in a manner of speaking, compulsive success-seekers. They are men of strength and intellect, courage and artistic inspiration, and there is a constructive stubbornness about them, a form of zeal, of persistence, of irrevocable faith in themselves and their projects, their ideas, their ideals, which ban any leave - taking of, or detour from, their committed path.

Such a man is Larry Steele, internationally renowned as the producer of the "Smart Affairs" revue, a production which is, in truth, "lavish with stars," "loaded with laughs," "sparkling with girls," and "rocking with rhythm." If the publicist who created those phrases is smug about his ability to zoom off into the literary wild, blue yonder, I must say—though it may be disillusioning—that he merely hit the target, dead-center. The "Smart Affairs" revue is all that and more. I know, I saw seventeen "Smart Affairs" shows in Las Vegas last year and, even so, I was disappointed when the production moved on; for six months thereafter, I caught myself humming tunes from the show every day; and I still see those lovely, dancing damsels in my dreams.

When you see Larry Steele on the stage, you see a star, meticulously groomed, handsome and debonair, a pro every tune (as a songwriter, he was recently made a member of ASCAP) and every step of the way. What you don't know is this: Larry Steele is not only producer and star, he is also his own self-secretary, bookkeeper, Father Confessor to the members of his troupe and—if we can believe what we read —a pretty good baker besides. "Larry Steele," said Ted Schall in the Atlantic City Press, "has mixed, blended, and baked an entertainment-rich cake which be serves up with a flourish..."

Larry Steele has been baking these cakes for 21 consecutive years. In spite of the vagaries of show business, including such as the "death" of vaudeville, the disappearance of the big bands of jazz, the emergence of rock 'n' roll, the intrusion of television, "Smart Affairs" has endured, through thick and thin, for all of this time... and has become an International Theatrical Institution.

Unless you've visited Larry Steele in his inner sanctum, you'd never guess that he's known thin times. But, he has, the very nature of his dream, his idea, his project—a production designed principally to glorify the beauty, the soul, and the talent of the Negro female—decreed that, crazy as it may sound while you're enjoying what you see, hard times were standard fare in this game.

Larry Steele

Naomi Williams, Pop William's Wife, pictured in the center with friends

Club Harlem Entertainers Gallery

Artists who performed at the Club from 1935-1985. These are the original portraits from the walls of the Walter D. Palmer Leadership School, Philadelphia, Pennsylvania.

Pearl Mae Bailey
March 29, 1918 – August 17, 1990

Pearl Bailey was a highly-acclaimed American actress and singer from Newport News, Virginia. Her first appearance on stage was when she was only 15 years old, and soon after won a singing competition at Harlem's famous Apollo Theater which launched her career in entertainment. Bailey performed nightclubs in vaudeville in the 1930s and toured the country with the USO during World II, until she made her Broadway debut in *St. Louis Woman* in 1946. She won a Tony Award for the title role in the all-Black production of *Hello, Dolly!* in 1968, where she starred alongside Cab Calloway. The Pearl Bailey Show aired on ABC between January and May of 1971, where she featured many notable guests in television and music. Her accolades include a Daytime Emmy award, a top ten hit, the Bronze Medallion in 1968, the Screen Actors Guild Life Achievement Award in 1976, and the Presidential Medal of Freedom from President Ronald Reagan.

Joseph Louis Barrow
May 13, 1914 – April 12, 1981

Known professionally as Joe Louis, he is considered to be one of the greatest American boxers of all times. From humble roots in Chamber County, Alabama, Louis achieved professional success in his career from 1934 to 1951. Nicknamed the "Brown Bomber" and renowned for his powerful punch, Louis only suffered 3 losses in 69 professional fights, maintained a championship reign of 140 consecutive months, during which he participated in 26 championship fights, and tallied 52 total knockouts.

Louis' cultural impact was felt well outside the ring. Within the United States, he is widely regarded as the first person of African-American descent to achieve the status of a nationwide hero, both for his accomplishments in and out of the boxing ring. In part, his recognition comes from his contribution in the Special Services Division of United States Army as a celebrity and focus of a media recruitment campaign to raise troop morale, denounce Nazism, and encourage African-American men to enlist in the Armed Services. His skill in the boxing ring and general legacy transcended racial lines.

Cabell "Cab" Calloway III
December 25, 1907 – November 18, 1994

Cab Calloway was an American jazz singer, dancer, and bandleader. Calloway was a master of energetic scat singing and a successful Broadway actor alongside Pearl Bailey in the all-Black production of *Hello, Dolly!* Most iconic was his leadership in one of the United States' most popular, "big bands" from the 1930's to the late 1940's. His musical jazz ensemble included trumpeters Dizzy Gillespie and Adolphus "Doc" Cheatham, saxophonists Ben Webster and Leon "Chu" Berry, guitarist Danny Barker, and bassist Milt Hinton. During this period Calloway had several hits, including his most famous song, "Minnie the Moocher," which was recorded in 1931. He was the first African American musician to sell a million records from a single song and to have a nationally syndicated radio show. Calloway also made several stage, film, and television appearances until his death in 1994 at the age of 86. He is in the Grammy Hall of Fame and received the Grammy Lifetime Achievement Award.

Nathaniel Adams Coles
March 17, 1919 – February 15, 1965

Nathaniel Adams Coles, known professionally as Nat King Cole, was an American vocalist and jazz pianist. He recorded over 100 songs that became hits on the pop charts. His musical trio, broadcasted as *King Cole Trio Time,* was the first radio program to be sponsored by an African American musician and is often credited as the model for small jazz ensembles that followed. Cole also acted in films, on television, and performed on Broadway. On November 5, 1956, the variety show *The Nat 'King' Cole Show* debuted on NBC with sponsorship from famous musical contemporaries like Ella Fitzgerald and Tony Bennett and was one of the first of its kind hosted by an African American.

William Boone Daniels
September 12, 1915 – October 7, 1988

William Boone Daniels, more commonly known as Billy Daniels, was a singer, entertainer, and actor famous throughout the United States and Europe in the mid-20th century. Early in his career he sang on New York radio for various sponsors and performed in nightclubs. Daniels was one of the first performers to leave the big-band scene and pursue a solo career, though he often had several accompanists when he played around New York City, including Nat King Cole and Benny Payne. His live performances were highly attended to hear his unique vocal stylings and see his trademark dance moves. His recording of "That Old Black Magic" was a signature at each performance. Later in his career he returned to New York to perform in musicals on Broadway, most notably in *Golden Boy* with Sammy Davis Jr. which ran for over 700 performances. Daniels also toured nationally with Pearl Bailey in the all-Black production of *Hello, Dolly!* and had his own television series on ABC in 1952 called *The Billy Daniels Show.* It was the first sponsored network television series starring a Black performer.

Samuel George Davis Jr.
December 8, 1925 – May 16, 1990

Sammy Davis Jr. was a highly popular American singer, musician, dancer, actor, vaudevillian, comedian, and activist, known in part for his inclusion in the Rat Pack with Frank Sinatra, Dean Martin, Peter Lawford and Joey Bishop. Also notable were his impressions of actors, musicians, and other celebrities in his live performances. Born in the Harlem neighborhood of New York City, Davis Jr. displayed a talent for entertainment at a very young age. He starred in a familial dance troupe called the Will Mastin Trio throughout his childhood, touring nationally and learning multiple instruments while on the road.

In 1955, his first two albums, *Starring Sammy Davis Jr.* and *Sammy Davis Jr. Sings Just for Lovers*, were released to both critical acclaim and commercial success, which in turn led to headlining performances in Las Vegas and New York. Davis Jr. refused to appear in any clubs that practiced racial segregation, leading to the integration of numerous high-profile venues across the United States. During the 1960s, he was also an advocate in the Civil Rights Movement, participating in the 1963 March on Washington.

Davis Jr.'s exciting career was filled with guest appearances on a wide variety of television shows, soap operas, and Broadway productions. In 1966, the entertainer hosted his own short-lived variety series, *The Sammy Davis Jr. Show.* His accolades include a Spingarn Medal by the NAACP, the Kennedy Center Honors, and the Grammy Lifetime Achievement Award.

William Clarence Eckstine
July 8, 1914 – March 8, 1993

Billy Eckstine was an influential band leader, jazz, and pop musician in the swing era. Born in Pittsburgh, Pennsylvania, Eckstine moved around a bit before settling in Chicago, Illinois, and joining an orchestra as a vocalist and trumpeter. Eckstine formed his own "bop big band" in 1944, which included young musicians like Dizzy Gilespie, Miles Davis, and many others that would later evolve the development of jazz. Eckstine's legacy, among many other accomplishments and qualities, was his rich, almost operatic bass-baritone voice.

Ella Jane Fitzgerald
April 25, 1917 – June 15, 1996

Ella Fitzgerald was an American jazz singer sometimes referred to as the First Lady of Song, Queen of Jazz, and Lady Ella. She was noted for her purity of tone, impeccable diction, phrasing, accuracy in pitch, and improvisational ability, particularly in her scat singing. After a tumultuous adolescence, Fitzgerald found stability in musical success with the Chick Webb Orchestra, performing across the country but most often associated with the Savoy Ballroom in Harlem. Her rendition of the nursery rhyme "A-Tisket, A-Tasket" helped boost both her to national fame. In 1942, Fitzgerald left the Orchestra to start her solo career. Under management from Norman Granz, who founded Verve Records, she recorded some of her more famous works, particularly her interpretations of the Great American Songbook.

While Fitzgerald appeared in movies and as a guest on popular television shows in the second half of the 20th century, her musical collaborations with Louis Armstrong, Duke Ellington, and The Ink Spots were some of her most notable acts outside of her solo career. These partnerships produced some of her best-known songs such as "Dream a Little Dream of Me," "Cheek to Cheek," "Into Each Life Some Rain Must Fall," and "It Don't Mean a Thing (If It Ain't Got That Swing)." Only a few of her many accomplishments and awards include 13 Grammy Awards, over 40 million albums sold, a National Medal of Arts, and the Presidential Medal of Freedom from President Ronald Reagan.

Richard Claxton Gregory
October 12, 1932 – August 19, 2017

Born in St. Louis, Missouri, Richard "Dick" Gregory was an American comedian, Civil Rights activist, social critic, writer, and occasional actor. During the 1960s, Gregory became a pioneer in stand-up comedy for his live sets, notorious for their daring and unrestricted nature in which Gregory ridiculed bigotry and racism. He performed primarily to Black audiences at segregated clubs until 1961, when he became the first Black comedian to successfully cross over to white audiences by appearing on television and putting out comedy record albums.

Gregory's legacy includes more than just his provocative comedic style and national acclaim. Equally as important was his position and leadership in political activism, especially of the 1960's when he protested the Vietnam War and racial injustice. During his lifetime, Gregory was arrested multiple times, went on many hunger strikes, and eventually became a public speaker and author.

Ruth Lee Jones
August 29, 1924 – December 14, 1963

Born in Tuscaloosa, Alabama, Ruth Lee Jones only went by her birth name until her teenage years when she began performing in clubs. While spending a year performing at the Garrick Stage Bar in Chicago, Illinois, owner Joe Sherman suggested the change to Dinah Washington. As an influential American singer and pianist, Washington has been cited as "the most popular Black female recording artist of the 1950s". Though her roots were in gospel music, her professional career was defined by performances and records in a wide variety of genres including blues, dirty blues, R&B, and pop music. Her notability was earned as a jazz vocalist. Between 1948 and 1955 Washington had 27 R&B top ten hits, making her one of the most commercially popular and successful singers of the period. Washington was a 1986 inductee of the Alabama Jazz Hall of Fame and was inducted into the Rock and Roll Hall of Fame in 1993.

Ray Charles Robinson
September 23, 1930 – June 10, 2004

Ray Charles was an American singer, songwriter, musician, and composer of many professional acclaims and an everlasting influencer on the music industry. Among friends and fellow musicians, he preferred being called "Brother Ray," but more generally has been referred to in the industry as "The Genius." Charles pioneered the soul music genre of the 1950s by combining blues, rhythm and blues, and gospel styles into his musical repertoire. He contributed to the integration of country music, rhythm and blues, and pop music during the 1960s with his crossover success between Atlantic and ABC Records, primarily with his two *Modern Sounds* albums. While he was with ABC, Charles became one of the first Black musicians to be granted artistic control by a mainstream record company. His combination of jazz, gospel, and R&B crafted a new genre of African American music known as soul. His accolades include designation by *Rolling Stone* as #10 on their list of the "100 Greatest Artists of All Time," and #2 on their list of the "100 Greatest Singers of All Time," in 2002 and 2008, respectively.

Larry Steele
1913 - June 19, 1980

Larry Steele gave a stage to Black musicians and dancers by supporting their careers and mentoring their craft, forever changing the entertainment world. Steele abandoned all thoughts of becoming a lawyer (pressure from his father) and dedicated himself to entertainment at a young age. He left Chicago, Illinois in the mid-1940s, helped organize entertainers on the Chitlin Circuit, and later found himself at Club Harlem in Atlantic City – the vanguard of entertainment on the east coast at the time. In the summer of 1946, Larry Steele opened his first Smart Affairs production at Club Harlem. Smart Affairs was a revue show featuring the best in African American music and the most talented and beautiful African American showgirls.

Smart Affairs and its associated acts spent the summer months entertaining the residents and tourists of Atlantic City. In its off season, Smart Affairs traveled the country. 1960, the Smart Affairs grossed between $400,000 and $500,000 annually and featured 40-50 performers who worked 40-45 hours per week. In commemoration of Steele's success, Howard University's Alumni Association presented him with the "Racial Dignity and Human Relations Award" in 1961. By 1969, Smart Affairs offered two simultaneous shows, one at Club Harlem and one at the Eden Roc Hotel in Miami Beach.

Larry Steele's Smart Affairs ran for 18 consecutive seasons at Club Harlem. Many famous African American performers had their start with, or appeared in, Steele's productions. Iconic performers at Club Harlem included Sammy Davis Jr., Sam Cooke, Aretha Franklin, Peg Leg Bates, Cab Calloway, Damita Jo, Slappy White, Sarah Vaughn, and Nat King Cole.

Sarah Lois Vaughan
March 27, 1924 – April 3, 1990

Nicknamed "Sassy" and "The Divine One," Sarah Vaughan was an American jazz vocalist and pianist. Vaughn's rich voice, three octave vocal range, and innovative improvisations earned her positions in jazz bands, touring both in the Unites States and Europe throughout the 1950's. She also appeared in three movies and appeared on television variety shows in her career. Among her best-known songs were "Lover Man" with Dizzy Gillespie and Charlie Parker, "It's Magic," "Make Yourself Comfortable," and "Broken-Hearted Melody." Some of Vaughan's many lifetime acclaims include a NEA Jazz Masters Award in 1989, induction into the Jazz Hall of Fame in 1990, and four Grammy Awards, including the Lifetime Achievement Award.

Paul Williams
December 1, 1934 – April 24, 2016

Known professionally as Billy Paul, Williams was a Grammy Award-winning American soul singer, known for his 1972 #1 single, "Me and Mrs. Jones" which topped the R&B and pop charts. Other famous records of the 1970s blended his more conventional pop, soul, and funk styles with electronic and psychedelic influences he became known for. Williams was one of the many artists associated with the Philadelphia soul sound, the city he was born in and found his love of music at a young age. Paul was identified by his diverse vocal style which ranged from mellow and soulful to low and raspy.

Stevland Hardaway Morris
May 13, 1950 –

Later altered to Stevland Morris when his mother married and better known by his stage name Stevie Wonder, he was born in Saginaw, Michigan in 1950. Wonder was completely blind soon after birth and quickly recognized as a child prodigy for his musical inclinations and talents. Before the age of nine, he was already singing in his church's choir and playing piano, drums, and harmonica. When he was only 12 years old, the owners of Motown Records offered him a recording contract and his professional music career took off. Less than a year later, "Little Stevie Wonder" as he was billed, earned his first US #1 single, *Fingertips.*

Wonder is widely regarded as a multi-talented American singer, songwriter, musician, and record producer that has transcended different styles and sounds of music in his long and illustrious career. As a prominent figure in popular music, Wonder is one of the most successful songwriters and critically acclaimed musicians of the 20th century. Through his pioneering heavy use of synthesizers, electronic instruments, and other innovative sounds, Wonder influenced musicians of various genres including R&B, jazz, reggae, soul, funk, pop, and rock & roll.

Special Thanks

A.S. "Doc" Young for the preserving the story of the Club Harlem and Smart Affairs.

Larry Steele for telling the original story of the Club Harlem.

Notice: This book in its entirety, along with other pictures from the Audrey Hart Collection, have been submitted to the National Museum of African American History in Washington D.C.

RESOLUTION OF THE CITY OF ATLANTIC CITY

No. 86

Council Member_____ALL COUNCIL_____Present the following Resolution:

RESOLUTION HONORING RICHARD (SKIP) ANDERSON, AUDREY (MISS AUDREY) HART AND ATLANTIC CITY AFRO'S BLACK POWER GROUP

WHEREAS, Atlantic City and Absecon Island were bought by White settlers for .04 to .40 cents per acre, from the Absegami and Lenape natives in the seventeen hundreds; and

WHEREAS, Atlantic City was incorporated by a young doctor Johnathan Pitney in 1854; and

WHEREAS, Blacks started to migrate to Atlantic City from the south before the end of the Civil War in 1864; and

WHEREAS, Atlantic City was racially segregated by Whites living on the south side towards the ocean and Blacks being segregated to the south side towards the Bay; and

WHEREAS, Blacks helped to build the hospitals, boardwalk and hotels, which they were not allowed to use; and

WHEREAS, in 1920, John Anderson, a shoemaker and his wife Thelma, who was a nurse, migrated from Churchill, Virginia to Atlantic City Kentucky Avenue; and

WHEREAS, they would have two sons, John (Buddy) and Richard (Skip) Anderson; and

WHEREAS, Richard (Skip) Anderson grew to become involved in the Civil Rights Movement in Detroit, Michigan and brought that experience back to Atlantic City; and

WHEREAS, in 1962, Audrey Hart, a twenty one year old professional dressmaker and third child of seven children to George and Ellen Hart of Hertford England; and

WHEREAS, Audrey would leave England at age twenty one and travel to Margate New Jersey to work as a nanny for the Malmut family, who were the owners of the Breakers and Shelborne hotels; and

WHEREAS, after a year Audrey will leave Margate and move to Atlantic City north side, which she called an oasis, and she meets Skip Anderson and after several years they will marry and have three sons, Omar, Abdullah and Tarik, who will have the first Arabic names in Atlantic City and they adopted a fourth child named Lamar Irby; and

WHEREAS, Skip Anderson and Audrey, who was named Miss Audrey by the Black Community of Atlantic City, organized the Black Afros in the 1960s, to fight against racial segregation in Atlantic City; and

WHEREAS, they fought against the commission form of government and would demonstrate and protest against the segregated schools, hospitals, telephone, public transportation, fire, police, post office, welfare, unions, banks, public works, coding, housing, courts, gas, electric, city lighting, sidewalk paving; and

WHEREAS, the Afros lead the way for the Institute on Human Development and laid the ground work for the first Black Mayor James Usry and eventually opened the doors for Blacks to be elected or appointed into every level of government; and

WHEREAS, Miss Audrey created the Afro Appearance, Tailoring and Thrift Shop over fifty years ago to start this movement and Miss Audrey continues to keep the movement alive through American, African and Atlantic City Black culture, history and community education.

NOW, THEREFORE BE IT RESOLVED that the Mayor and City Council of Atlantic City give recognition to Richard (Skip) Anderson, Miss Audrey, the Atlantic City Black Afro's Organization and all of those who fought to make Atlantic City a better place for everyone.

ORIGINAL MEMBERS ATLANTIC CITY BLACK AFROS

Richard Skip Anderson ● Audrey Hart Anderson ● Freddy Johnson ● Sam Giles ● Andy Anderson ● Tanya Wyatt ● Pat Patterson Israel Mosse ● Barbara Monroe ● Chris Columbo ● Iron Head Cash ● Tim Tam Cash ● Jimmy Bradley ● Otis Williams ● Harold Nuky Johnson George Powell ● Bobby Jackson ● Doris Sewell ● Quince the Barber ● Hannah Mosse ● Barbara Gilliam ● Dr. Juanita Hyatt

DO NOT USE SPACE BELOW THIS LINE												
RECORD OF COUNCIL VOTE ON FINAL PASSAGE												
COUNCIL MEMBER	AYE	NAY	N.V	A.B.	MOT.	SEC.	COUNCIL MEMBER	AYE	NAY	N.V.	A.B.	MOT.	SEC.
DELGADO	X				X	X	MORSHED	X				X	X
DUNSTON	X				X	X	RANDOLPH	X				X	X
FAUNTLEROY	X				X	X	SHABAZZ	X				X	X
KURTZ	X				X	X	ZIA	X				X	X
							TIBBITT, PRESIDENT	X				X	X

X-Indicates Vote   NV-Not Voting   AB-Absent   MOT-Motion   SEC-Second

This is a Certified True copy of the Original Resolution on file in the City Clerk's Office.

DATE OF ADOPTION: _____FEBRUARY 19, 2020_____   *Paula Geletei*

/s/ Paula Geletei, City Clerk

In Memoriam

To all the Atlantic City Afros who lived, fought, and died fighting
for the social justice in Atlantic City, New Jersey.

Richard "Skip" Anderson (Father)
Co-founder of Atlantic City Afros

12/19/1937 – 11/12/2010

Omar Ahmed Anderson (Son)
Master Barber

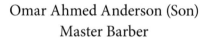

7/26/1968 – 1/11/2011

Amar Anderson Davenport (Grandson)
Angel

10/15/2017 – 6/12/2018

Public Appeal

The Palmer Foundation is a federal 501(c)(3) organization that has spent over 65 years educating and fighting for social justice in the most underserved at-risk communities around the country. Our goals have always been to use education for human liberation and encourage at-risk families and children to help gather, write, produce, publish, and teach others in a similar situation.

Our mission is to disseminate our leadership, self-development, social justice, and grassroots-organizing books, manuals, and learning materials across America and around the world. We prefer not to sell these publications, but rather offer them in exchange for a suggested tax-exempt donation that would allow us to continue producing our leadership training, as well as grassroots community and political organizing efforts.

About the Artist

Cavin Jones is a painter and muralist from Philadelphia. He received his Bachelor of Fine Arts in Painting from the Tyler School of Art in Elkins Park, Pennsylvania. He then went on to receive his Master of Fine Arts in Painting from Washington University in St. Louis, Missouri.

He has a unique style, including collage, which he says allows him to distill his various ideas and interests into a single painting. Cavin sees his work as a way to stimulate dialogue about issues surrounding race and environmentalism. He has been featured in many prestigious collections and exhibitions. Cavin's art is inspired by American history, environmental exploitation, and the African American experience.

My Life in The Sunshine
Colored pencil, gouache, marker, collage on paper
34" x 26"
1987

A Brief Biography of Professor Walter Palmer

———●———

After a tumultuous juvenile life, Professor Palmer graduated from high school and was hired by the University of Pennsylvania hospital as a surgical attendant and eventually was recruited into the University of Pennsylvania School of Inhalation and Respiratory (Oxygen) Therapy.

After his certification as an inhalation and respiratory therapist, he was hired by the Children's Hospital of Philadelphia as the Director of the Department of Inhalation and Respiratory (Oxygen) Therapy, where he spent ten years helping to develop the national field of cardio-pulmonary therapy.

Professor Palmer has also pursued further education at Temple University for Business Administration and Communications, Cheyney State University for a Teacher's Degree in History and Secondary Education. And at age 40, acquired his juris doctorate in law from Howard University.

In 2006, he was inducted into the Philadelphia College of Physicians as a Fellow for the body of work he had done over the past 70 years.

During that entire period, Professor Palmer led the Civil Rights, Black Power and Afrocentric movements in Philadelphia, around the country as well as Caribbean and West Indies.

In the 1980s to 2015, he led the school choice movement and in 2000 had the Walter D. Palmer School named after him.

In 1962, he created a school without walls on the University of Pennsylvania's campus and became a visiting lecturer in the Schools of Medicine, Law, Education, Wharton, History, Africana Studies, Engineering, and he currently is a lecturer in the Schools of Medicine, Social Work, and Urban Studies, where he teaches courses on American racism.

In 1969, he helped the Graduate School of Social Work create required courses on American racism, making the University of Pennsylvania, the first school in American academia to have such courses.

Over his many years of teaching, he has received the title of Teacher Par Excellence and has amassed several hundred medals, trophies, plaques, certificates, and awards for his active participation in multiple disciplines.

Contact Us

The W.D. Palmer Foundation (1955)

PO Box 26629

Philadelphia, PA 19110

267-738-1588

thewdpalmerfoundation@gmail.com

https://www.speakerservices.com/walter-d-palmer/

(Black Bottom)

(Black Revolution)

(Black Studies)

(Black Power)

W.D. Palmer Publishing

A wholly owned subsidiary of the W.D. Palmer Foundation

Please inquire about projects under construction:

Who Were the Original Indigenous Natives of the World and What Happened to Them?

Africa's Gift to the World: The African Diaspora

Everything You Must Know Before Starting a Dialogue on Racism

The Little Black Boy Who Dared to Lead

Age of Justice (Real Life Comic Hero) W.D. Palmer

W.D. Palmer Urban Leadership (K-12) Curriculum

Walter D Palmer Leadership School

W. D. Palmer Foundation Hashtags

1. #racedialogueusa
2. #racismdialogueusa
3. #atriskchildrenusa
4. #youthorganizingusa
5. #stopblackonblackusa
6. #newleadershipusa
7. #liberationeducationusa
8. #sixteennineteenusa
9. #1619usa
10. #africanslaveryusa
11. #indigenouspeopleusa
12. #panafricanusa
13. #afrocentricusa
14. #africanausa
15. #civillibertiesusa
16. #civilrightsusa
17. #humanrightsusa

Printed in the United States
By Bookmasters